The Cornerstones of Health and Wellness

By Zach Dirr

ELITE LAB
STIX

Elite Performance
765.499.1005
eliteptindy.com
elitelabstix@gmail.com

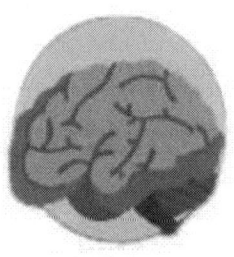

BRAIN HEALTH
Training your brain has overarching health benefits we're still discovering every day, month, and year.

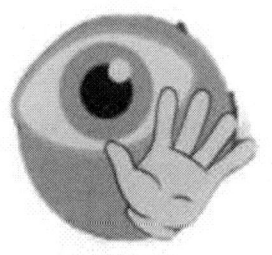

EYE HAND COORDINATION
Improved coordination between what we see and how our body responds all starts with our vision.

FOCUS
Studies have shown that improved vision teaming and efficiency can lead to improved and prolonged concentration

CREATIVITY
Creating new and different neural connections in the brain allow for increased amounts of creativity.

REACTION TIME
The time it takes for you to see something, process that information, and respond to it can be greatly improved.

SAFETY
Increased sports vision training skills lead to improved field/sport awareness leading to improved safety.

ELITE INNOVATIONS
BUILDING TOMORROW'S FUTURE TODAY

Copyright 2024 by Zach Dirr

All Rights Reserved.

No part of this publication may be reproduced, distributed, or transmitted in any form of by any means, including photocopying, recording, or other electronic methods, without the prior written permission of the publisher, except in the case of brief quotations embodied in critical reviews and certain other non-commercial uses permitted by copyright law.

Table of Contents

Introduction 1

Chapter 1: The Significance of Cognitive Health in Overall Well-being 5

Chapter 2: Understanding the Brain: Exploring Structure and Function 10

Chapter 3: The Modern Health Crisis: Addressing the Rise in Chronic Diseases 18

Chapter 4: Exploring Neuro-Cognitive Training: Techniques, Approaches, and Scientific Support 26

Chapter 5: The Mind-Body Connection: Bridging Mental and Physical Health 35

Chapter 6: Nutrition and Brain Health: Nourishing the Mind for Optimal Function 43

Chapter 7: Enhancing Cognitive Fitness: The Synergistic Impact of Physical Activity and Cognitive Training 52

Chapter 8: Sleep and Brain Restoration: Unlocking the Power of Quality Rest 61

Chapter 9: Cognitive Customization for Healthier Longevity 70

Chapter 10: Integrating Cognitive Training into Your Life 76

Chapter 11: Success Stories 84

Chapter 12: Impact of Health Avenue Technologies 86

Conclusion 88

Introduction

Nurturing Cognitive Health for Holistic Well-being

In the intricate tapestry of human existence, the significance of cognitive health stands as a linchpin, weaving its influence through the fabric of our overall well-being.

Cognitive health, encapsulating the vitality of our mental processes, extends beyond mere cognitive prowess, encompassing memory, problem-solving abilities, emotional regulation, and social interactions. Understanding its profound implications is tantamount to recognizing the intricate dance between mental and physical dimensions, forming the essence of holistic well-being.

The Significance of Cognitive Health in Overall Well-being

Cognitive health, often the unsung hero in discussions of well-being, plays a pivotal role in shaping the quality of our lives. It is the compass guiding our thoughts, the guardian of our memories, and the architect of our decision-making processes. From the mundane to the extraordinary, cognitive health is the silent orchestrator, influencing our ability to learn, adapt, and navigate the complexities of the human experience. Its significance extends beyond individual realms, impacting the harmony of communities, societies, and the broader human collective.

The Purpose and Scope of Being Healthy

Being healthy transcends the mere absence of illness; it embodies a dynamic equilibrium across physical, mental, and social dimensions. The purpose of being healthy lies in the optimization of one's potential — a vibrant synergy between a resilient body and a thriving mind. This holistic approach to health acknowledges the interconnectedness of various facets, where physical well-being empowers mental vitality, and vice versa.

The scope of being healthy extends beyond personal aspirations to encompass the creation of communities and societies that nurture the well-being of all, fostering an environment where individuals can flourish in unison.

As we delve into the intricacies of cognitive health and the broader purpose of being healthy, we embark on a journey toward a nuanced understanding of well-being—one that embraces the profound interplay between mind and body, individual and community, and the intricate threads that weave the tapestry of a fulfilling and resilient life.

SENSORY PERFORMANCE REPORT
RED. OVERALL SCORE 59

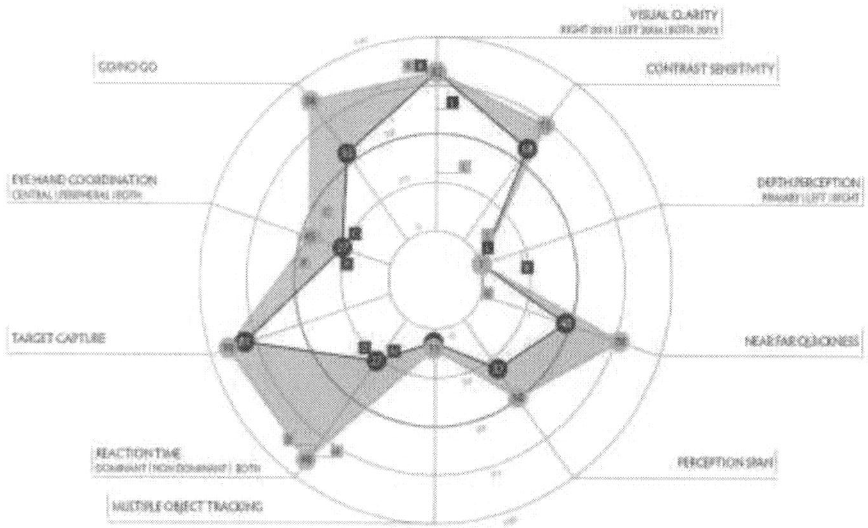

KEY

- FIRST EVALUATION — 11/28/2023 @ 12:29
- SECOND EVALUATION — 06/03/2022 @ 14:33
- AREA OF INCREASE
- PERCENTILE

Chart axes:
- TARGET CAPTURE
- EYE-HAND COORDINATION (CENTRAL / PERIPHERAL / BOTH)
- GO/NO GO
- VISUAL CLARITY (RIGHT 20/20 | LEFT 20/20 | BOTH 20/20)
- CONTRAST SENSITIVITY
- DEPTH PERCEPTION (PRIMARY / LEFT / RIGHT)
- NEAR FAR QUICKNESS
- PERCEPTION SPAN
- REACTION TIME (DOMINANT / NON DOMINANT / BOTH)
- MULTIPLE OBJECT TRACKING

OTHER SPORT:
N/A

POSITION:
N/A

HEIGHT:
5'11"

OTHER CURRENT LEVEL:

COMPARED TO:

STRENGTHS
- TARGET CAPTURE

OPPORTUNITIES
- DEPTH PERCEPTION
- GO/NO GO
- REACTION TIME
- NEAR FAR QUICKNESS
- MULTIPLE OBJECT TRACKING
- EYE HAND COORDINATION
- PERCEPTION SPAN

PRESCRIPTION PLAN
- DEPTH PERCEPTION
- STROBE EYEWEAR
- SENSORY STATION
- PERCEPTION TRAINING

SENAPTEC

Chapter 1
The Significance of Cognitive Health in Overall Well-being

In the intricate tapestry of human well-being, cognitive health stands as a crucial thread, weaving its influence across various aspects of our lives. Cognitive health encompasses the functionality of our brain, including processes such as memory, problem-solving, and decision-making. Understanding its significance requires delving into its impact on both individual and collective well-being.

The Interconnectedness of Cognitive Health

Cognitive health serves as the cornerstone of our ability to navigate the complexities of daily life. From the simplest tasks to the most complex challenges, our cognitive faculties play a pivotal role. Memory, for instance, allows us to learn from past experiences, while effective problem-solving skills empower us to tackle new obstacles.

Moreover, cognitive health extends beyond the individual, influencing social dynamics and relationships. Empathy, communication, and interpersonal skills, all rooted in cognitive processes, shape the quality of our connections with others. As such, a society with robust cognitive health is better equipped to foster understanding, collaboration, and collective growth.

The Lifelong Journey of Cognitive Well-being

Unlike static components of well-being, cognitive health is dynamic and subject to change. It is a lifelong journey influenced by genetics, lifestyle choices, and environmental factors. Nurturing cognitive well-being involves adopting habits that support brain health, such as regular exercise, a balanced diet, and mental stimulation.

Continuous cognitive development contributes not only to the individual's adaptability but also to the resilience of communities. A society that values and invests in the cognitive well-being of its members creates a foundation for innovation, productivity, and overall progress.

Purpose and Scope of Being Healthy

The pursuit of health is a multifaceted journey that extends far beyond the absence of illness. It encompasses physical, mental, and social well-being, intertwining these elements to create a holistic sense of vitality. The purpose of being healthy is not merely the absence of disease but the optimization of one's potential across various domains.

- **Physical Well-being**
  A healthy body is a vehicle for an active and fulfilling life. Physical health provides the energy and resilience needed to engage in daily activities, pursue passions, and navigate the world with vitality.

- **Mental Well-being**
  Mental health is the bedrock of cognitive and emotional resilience. It involves fostering positive thoughts, managing stress, and cultivating a mindset that supports overall happiness and fulfillment.

- **Social Well-being**
  Human beings are inherently social creatures, and our well-being is intricately tied to the quality of our connections. Social health involves building and maintaining supportive relationships, fostering a sense of belonging, and contributing to the well-being of the broader community.

Embracing a Holistic Perspective

In conclusion, the significance of cognitive health in overall well-being is profound and interconnected. Recognizing the purpose and scope of being healthy involves embracing a holistic perspective that considers the intricate interplay between physical, mental, and social well-being. By nurturing cognitive health and adopting a comprehensive approach to well-being, individuals and societies can unlock their full potential and thrive in the tapestry of life.

SENSORY PERFORMANCE REPORT
ORANGE. OVERALL SCORE 13

SENAPTEC

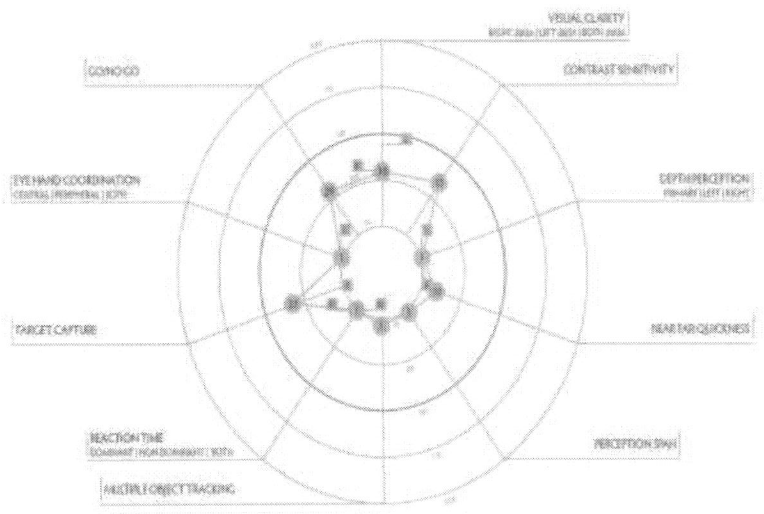

SPORT
AUTO RACING

POSITION
KART

HEIGHT

CURRENT LEVEL
MIDDLE SCHOOL

COMPARED TO
MIDDLE SCHOOL
DYNAMIC

STRENGTHS
CONTRAST SENSITIVITY
TARGET CAPTURE
GO/NO GO
VISUAL CLARITY

OPPORTUNITIES
REACTION TIME
DEPTH PERCEPTION
EYE HAND COORDINATION
PERCEPTION SPAN

PRESCRIPTION PLAN
EYE EXAM RECOMMENDED
NEAR FAR SHIFT
DEPTH PERCEPTION
PERCEPTION TRAINING

KEY

FIRST EVALUATION
08/11/2022 @ 22:14

AREA OF INCREASE

PERCENTILE

Chart labels: VISUAL CLARITY, CONTRAST SENSITIVITY, DEPTH PERCEPTION, NEAR FAR QUICKNESS, PERCEPTION SPAN, MULTIPLE OBJECT TRACKING, REACTION TIME, TARGET CAPTURE, EYE HAND COORDINATION, GO/NO GO

Chapter 2

Understanding the Brain: Exploring Structure and Function

Unraveling the Complexity: Exploring the Structure of the Brain

Understanding the brain is akin to deciphering an intricate code that holds the key to our thoughts, emotions, and actions. At its core, the brain is a marvel of biological engineering, composed of billions of nerve cells called neurons. These neurons form an elaborate network, communicating through electrical and chemical signals to orchestrate the symphony of human experience.

1. The Brain's Architectural Wonders

The brain comprises distinct regions, each with specialized functions. The cerebral cortex, responsible for higher cognitive functions, is divided into lobes such as the frontal, parietal, temporal, and occipital lobes. Deeper structures, including the hippocampus and amygdala, play vital roles in memory and emotional processing.

2. Neural Communication

Neurons communicate through synapses, where neurotransmitters bridge the gaps between cells. This intricate dance of chemical messengers forms the basis of learning, memory, and myriad cognitive processes.

3. Plasticity and Adaptability

One of the brain's most remarkable features is its plasticity—the ability to reorganize and adapt. This capacity allows the brain to form new neural connections, learn from experiences, and recover from injuries.

The Symphony of Function: Understanding the Brain's Role in Cognitive Health

1. Cognitive Health and Physical Well-being

The connection between cognitive health and physical health is profound, reflecting the symbiotic relationship between the brain and the body. Physical exercise, for example, not only enhances cardiovascular health but also promotes neurogenesis—the creation of new neurons—and improves cognitive functions.

2. Neurotransmitters and Mental Well-being

The brain's chemical messengers, neurotransmitters, play a pivotal role in mental well-being. Imbalances in neurotransmitter levels are implicated in various mental health conditions, emphasizing the importance of maintaining a neurochemically balanced brain for optimal cognitive function.

3. Sleep and Brain Restoration

Adequate sleep is crucial for cognitive health, as it allows the brain to consolidate memories, repair cellular damage, and regulate neurotransmitter levels. Chronic sleep deprivation, conversely, can impair cognitive function and contribute to mental health challenges.

4. Nutrition and Cognitive Well-being

The brain's intricate functions rely on a steady supply of nutrients. Diets rich in antioxidants, omega-3 fatty acids, and other essential nutrients support brain health, promoting cognitive resilience and reducing the risk of cognitive decline.

Cultivating Cognitive Resilience: A Holistic Approach

Understanding the brain involves recognizing the interplay between its structure, function, and the broader context of physical health. By adopting a holistic approach that encompasses regular exercise, adequate sleep, and a nourishing diet, individuals can cultivate cognitive resilience and promote overall well-being.

The intricate interplay between cognitive health and physical well-being underscores the profound impact that mental fitness can have on the body. As research continues to unveil the Intricate connections between the mind and body, it becomes increasingly evident that cognitive health plays a pivotal role in shaping and maintaining physical health.

One of the key mechanisms through which cognitive health influences physical well- being is stress management. A healthy mind is better equipped to cope with stressors, preventing the harmful physiological effects of chronic stress on the body.

Stress reduction, facilitated by robust cognitive health, contributes to a lower risk of cardiovascular issues, improved immune function, and enhanced overall resilience.

Additionally, cognitive health influences lifestyle choices, such as diet and exercise. A well-functioning brain exhibits better decision-making abilities, leading to healthier food choices and increased motivation for physical activity. Conversely, cognitive impairments may contribute to sedentary behavior and poor dietary habits, which are known risk factors for various health conditions.

Furthermore, cognitive health is closely linked to sleep quality. Adequate and restorative sleep is crucial for physical health, as it supports cellular repair, immune function, and overall vitality. Cognitive functions such as attention, memory consolidation, and emotional regulation contribute to a healthy sleep routine.
Conversely, sleep disturbances associated with cognitive issues can negatively impact physical health, increasing susceptibility to chronic conditions.

The mind-body connection is further exemplified in the role of cognitive health in pain perception and management. A resilient mind can better modulate pain signals, leading to improved pain tolerance and coping mechanisms. In contrast, cognitive impairments may exacerbate the perception of pain, hindering one's ability to engage in physical activities and negatively impacting overall quality of life.

Moreover, cognitive health influences habits related to substance use and abuse. A sound mental state enhances decision-making abilities, reducing the likelihood of engaging in harmful behaviors such as excessive alcohol consumption or substance abuse. Conversely, cognitive impairments may compromise judgment, leading to detrimental health consequences.

The symbiotic relationship between cognitive health and physical well-being underscores the importance of nurturing both aspects for overall health. A healthy mind not only contributes to enhanced stress resilience, better lifestyle choices, and improved sleep but also plays a crucial role in pain perception and substance use behaviors. Recognizing and addressing the connections between cognitive and physical health is integral to fostering holistic well-being and empowering individuals to lead healthier, more fulfilling lives.

In conclusion, the journey to understand the brain is a voyage into the depths of human complexity. Exploring the brain's structure unveils its architectural wonders, while understanding its function reveals the intricate symphony of cognitive processes. Recognizing the intimate link between cognitive and physical health empowers individuals to navigate this intricate landscape, fostering a harmonious balance that sustains the mind and body alike.

SENSORY PERFORMANCE REPORT
YELLOW • OVERALL SCORE 24

SENAPTEC

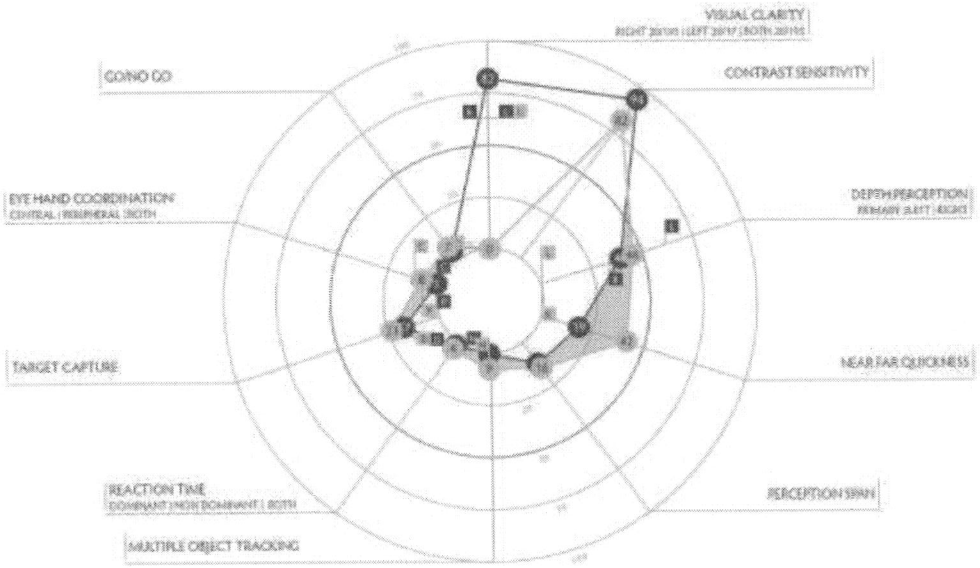

SPORT
POSITION AUTO RACING
HEIGHT KART
CURRENT LEVEL 4'1"

COMPARED TO MIDDLE SCHOOL

STRENGTHS
MIDDLE SCHOOL
DYNAMIC

OPPORTUNITIES
CONTRAST SENSITIVITY
DEPTH PERCEPTION
NEAR FAR QUICKNESS
TARGET CAPTURE
PRESCRIPTION PLAN
REACTION TIME
VISUAL CLARITY
MULTIPLE OBJECT TRACKING
GO/NO GO

KEY

FIRST EVALUATION 08/11/2022 @ 21:30
SECOND EVALUATION 05/05/2022 @ 22:02

AREA OF INCREASE

PERCENTILE

Chart axes:
- EYE-HAND COORDINATION (CENTRAL, PERIPHERAL, BOTH)
- TARGET CAPTURE
- REACTION TIME (DOMINANT HAND, SUBDOMINANT, BOTH)
- MULTIPLE OBJECT TRACKING
- PERCEPTION SPAN
- NEAR FAR QUICKNESS
- DEPTH PERCEPTION (NEAR IN 3 FT, 40 IN)
- CONTRAST SENSITIVITY
- VISUAL CLARITY (RIGHT 20/16, LEFT 20/17, BOTH 20/16)
- GO/NO GO

Chapter 3

The Modern Health Crisis: Addressing the Rise in Chronic Diseases

The intricate relationship between cognitive decline and chronic illnesses sheds light on the multifaceted nature of health, with cognitive impairment often playing a significant role in the progression and management of various long-term health conditions.

One prominent connection exists between cognitive decline and chronic diseases, particularly those affecting the cardiovascular system. Conditions such as hypertension and diabetes, when poorly managed, can lead to vascular damage, impacting blood flow to the brain. This vascular compromise contributes to cognitive decline, with research suggesting a higher risk of conditions like dementia among individuals with uncontrolled chronic diseases.

Furthermore, chronic inflammation, a hallmark of many long-term illnesses, is closely linked to cognitive decline. Inflammatory processes can affect the brain, contributing to the development of neurodegenerative disorders. Conditions like Alzheimer's disease and Parkinson's disease have been associated with chronic inflammation, emphasizing the intricate interplay between systemic health and cognitive function.

Diabetes, in particular, stands out as a chronic illness with a significant impact on cognitive health. Uncontrolled blood sugar levels can lead to damage in blood vessels throughout the body, including those in the brain. This vascular damage increases the risk of cognitive decline and the development of conditions such as vascular dementia.

The psychological aspects of living with chronic illnesses also contribute to cognitive decline. The mental burden of managing a long-term condition, coping with symptoms, and facing uncertainties about the future can lead to increased stress, anxiety, and depression. These mental health challenges, if left unaddressed, can contribute to cognitive impairment over time.

Medication side effects, often a part of chronic illness management, may also play a role in cognitive decline. Some medications have been associated with cognitive impairment or an increased risk of conditions like dementia. Striking a delicate balance between managing chronic illnesses and minimizing potential cognitive side effects poses a challenge in the comprehensive care of individuals with long-term health conditions.

Cognitive decline and chronic illnesses share intricate connections that significantly impact an individual's overall well-being. The vascular, inflammatory, psychological, and pharmacological factors involved highlight the need for a holistic approach to healthcare. Integrating cognitive health assessments and interventions into the management of chronic diseases is crucial for promoting not only physical health but also cognitive vitality. Recognizing and addressing cognitive decline in the context of chronic illnesses is essential for enhancing the quality of life and long-term outcomes for individuals navigating the complex landscape of chronic health conditions.

The Alarming Escalation of Chronic Diseases

The modern era is marked by remarkable advancements, yet it bears witness to an escalating health crisis characterized by the surge in chronic diseases. These conditions, including heart disease, diabetes, and mainly respiratory disorders, pose a significant threat to global well-being. Understanding the roots of this crisis is essential for devising effective strategies to mitigate its impact.

1. Lifestyle Factors and Chronic Diseases

The rise in chronic diseases is intricately linked to modern lifestyles. Sedentary habits, poor dietary choices, and increased stress contribute to the prevalence of conditions that were once relatively rare. Addressing this crisis requires a shift towards healthier living habits.

2. The Need for Preventive Measures

A crucial aspect of tackling chronic diseases is prioritizing preventive measures. Educating individuals about the importance of regular exercise, balanced nutrition, and stress management can significantly reduce the risk of developing these conditions.

Addressing the Rise in Chronic Diseases: Strategies for Improvement

1. Public Health Initiatives

Governments and health organizations play a pivotal role in addressing the modern health crisis. Implementing public health initiatives focused on education, preventive care, and accessible healthcare can empower communities to make informed choices about their well-being.

2. Technological Innovations in Healthcare

Embracing technological advancements can enhance healthcare delivery. From telemedicine for remote consultations to wearable devices that monitor health metrics, technology provides tools to track and manage chronic conditions effectively.

3. Holistic Approaches to Healthcare

Shifting towards holistic healthcare models that consider both physical and mental well-being is crucial. Integrating mental health support into routine healthcare can address the interconnected nature of physical and mental health.

The Role of Cognitive Decline in Chronic Illnesses

1. Bidirectional Relationship

Cognitive decline and chronic illnesses share a bidirectional relationship. Chronic conditions, particularly those affecting the cardiovascular system, can contribute to cognitive decline.

Conversely, cognitive decline may impede an individual's ability to manage their health effectively.

2. Impact on Adherence to Treatment
Cognitive decline can affect a person's ability to adhere to medical recommendations and treatment plans. This challenges the effectiveness of interventions for chronic diseases, emphasizing the need for personalized and supportive healthcare strategies.

3. Stress and Cognitive Health
Chronic illnesses often induce stress, which, in turn, can exacerbate cognitive decline. Developing stress management techniques becomes integral not only for mental health but also for mitigating the impact on chronic conditions.

Toward a Healthier Future

In conclusion, addressing the modern health crisis requires a multifaceted approach that considers lifestyle factors, preventive measures, and the intricate interplay between cognitive decline and chronic illnesses. By fostering a collective commitment to healthier living, leveraging technological innovations, and embracing holistic healthcare models, society can pave the way for a healthier future—one where chronic diseases are not just treated but prevented, and cognitive well-being is prioritized as an integral part of overall health.

SENSORY PERFORMANCE REPORT
GREEN. OVERALL SCORE 55

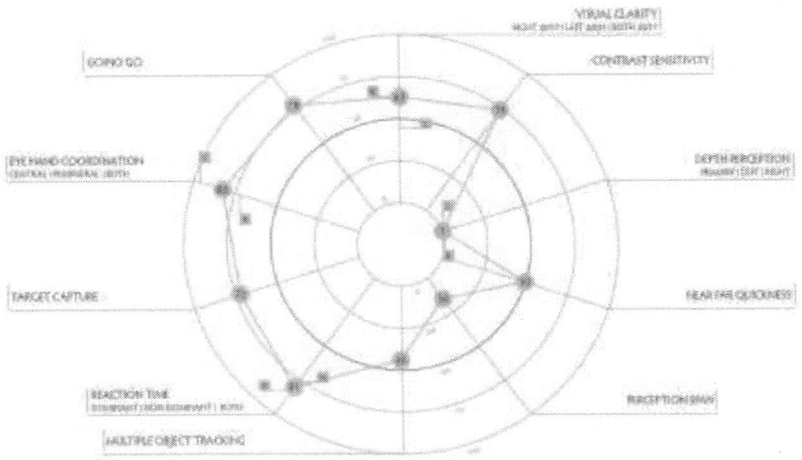

SPORT
AUTO RACING

POSITION
KART

HEIGHT
4'10"

CURRENT LEVEL
MIDDLE SCHOOL

COMPARED TO
MIDDLE SCHOOL
DYNAMIC

STRENGTHS
EYE HAND COORDINATION
REACTION TIME
GO/NO GO
CONTRAST SENSITIVITY

OPPORTUNITIES
DEPTH PERCEPTION
PERCEPTION SPAN
VISUAL CLARITY
MULTIPLE OBJECT TRACKING

PRESCRIPTION PLAN
DEPTH PERCEPTION
PERCEPTION TRAINING
STROBE EYEWEAR
DYNAMIC VISION

SENAPTEC

KEY

FIRST EVALUATION
12/19/2022 @ 21:59

AREA OF INCREASE

PERCENTILE

Chart axes:
- EYE HAND COORDINATION
- TARGET CAPTURE
- REACTION TIME
- MULTIPLE OBJECT TRACKING
- PERCEPTION SPAN
- DEPTH PERCEPTION
- CONTRAST SENSITIVITY
- VISUAL CLARITY
- GO/NO GO

Chapter 4

Exploring Neuro-Cognitive Training: Techniques, Approaches, and Scientific Support

Unraveling Neuro-Cognitive Training

In the realm of cognitive enhancement, neurocognitive training emerges as a dynamic and evolvingfield designed to optimize brain function. This training encompasses a range of techniques and approaches aimed at improving cognitive abilities, such as memory, attention, and problem-solving skills.

1. **Cognitive Training Techniques**
   - Working Memory Training: This technique focuses on enhancing the capacity to hold and manipulate information in the short term, aiding tasks requiring mental agility.
   - Attention Training: Designed to improve sustained attention and the ability to filter out distractions, attention training is beneficial for tasks that demand prolonged

focus.
- Brain Games and Apps: Various computerized programs and mobile applications offer gamified exercises targeting specific cognitive functions. These often involve puzzles, memory challenges, and problem-solving activities.

2. Brain Stimulation Approaches
- Transcranial Direct Current Stimulation (tDCS): This non-invasive technique involves applying a low electrical current to specific areas of the brain. Research suggests that tDCS may enhance learning and cognitive performance.
- Neurofeedback: Individuals receive real-time information about their brain activity and learn to regulate it. Neurofeedback is used to address conditions like ADHD and anxiety by training the brain to achieve more optimal patterns of activity.

3. Mindfulness and Meditation
- Mindfulness-Based Cognitive Therapy (MBCT): Integrating mindfulness practices with cognitive therapy, MBCT has shown efficacy in preventing the

recurrence of depression and reducing stress. Mindfulness meditation is associated with improvements in attention and emotional regulation.

Scientific Evidence Supporting Effectiveness

1. Working Memory Training
- Research by Jaeggi et al. (2008): A seminal study suggested that working memory training can lead to significant improvements not only in working memory itself but also in fluid intelligence—the ability to solve novel problems.

2. Attention Training
- The ACTIVE Study (2017): The Advanced Cognitive Training for Independent and Vital Elderly (ACTIVE) study demonstrated that attention training interventions led to long-term improvements in cognitive function, particularly in older adults.

3. Brain Stimulation Approaches
- Kuo et al. (2016): A study exploring tDCS found that this technique could enhance cognitive performance, with specific effects

on working memory and attention.

4. **Mindfulness and Meditation**
   - Tang et al. (2015): Research indicates that mindfulness meditation can induce structural changes in the brain, particularly in areas associated with self- awareness, compassion, and introspection.

Navigating the Future of Neuro-Cognitive Training

While the field of neuro-cognitive training shows promise, it is essential to approach it with a nuanced understanding. Individual responses can vary, and the effectiveness of specific techniques may depend on factors such as age, baseline cognitive abilities, and the targeted cognitive domain.

As neuroscientists and researchers continue to explore and refine neuro-cognitive training methodologies, the integration of personalized approaches, comprehensive assessments, and ongoing scientific inquiry will be instrumental in unlocking the full potential of cognitive enhancement. The journey to understand and harness the power of neuro-cognitive training holds exciting prospects for individuals seeking to optimize their cognitive capabilities and lead mentally resilient lives.

Enhancing neurocognitive function is a pursuit that encompasses a range of techniques and strategies aimed at optimizing brain health and cognitive abilities. From lifestyle choices to targeted interventions, these approaches contribute to improved memory, attention, and overall cognitive performance.

1. Physical Exercise

Regular physical activity has been consistently linked to cognitive benefits. Exercise increases blood flow to the brain, promotes the growth of new neurons, and enhances the release of neurotransmitters that support cognitive function. Aerobic exercises, such as running or swimming, are particularly effective in promoting brain health.

2. Healthy Diet

Proper nutrition is fundamental to cognitive well-being. Diets rich in antioxidants, omega-3 fatty acids, and other nutrients support brain function and protect against cognitive decline. Foods like fatty fish, berries, nuts, and leafy greens have been associated with cognitive benefits.

3. Mental Stimulation

Engaging in intellectually stimulating activities helps keep the brain active and agile. Activities such as reading, solving puzzles, learning new skills, and engaging in hobbies that require cognitive effort contribute to the establishment of cognitive reserves, which can buffer against age-related decline.

4. Adequate Sleep

Quality sleep is crucial for cognitive health. During sleep, the brain consolidates memories, eliminates toxins, and undergoes essential repair processes. Chronic sleep deprivation has been linked to impaired cognitive function, emphasizing the importance of prioritizing a good night's sleep.

5. Stress Management

Chronic stress can have detrimental effects on the brain. Stress-reduction techniques such as mindfulness meditation, yoga, and deep breathing exercises promote relaxation and have been associated with improvements in attention, memory, and overall cognitive function.

6. Social Engagement

Maintaining social connections is beneficial for cognitive health. Regular social interactions stimulate the brain, enhance emotional well-being, and provide opportunities for intellectual engagement. Strong social networks have been linked to a reduced risk of cognitive decline.

7. Cognitive Training

Specific cognitive exercises and training programs are designed to target and improve particular cognitive functions. These programs often involve tasks that challenge memory, attention, and problem-solving skills. While results may vary, some studies suggest that cognitive training can lead to positive cognitive outcomes, especially in older adults.

8. Brain-Boosting Supplements

Certain dietary supplements, such as omega-3 fatty acids, vitamins, and antioxidants, are believed to support brain health. However, it's essential to approach supplementation with caution and consult with healthcare professionals to ensure safety and efficacy.

9. Learning and Education

Lifelong learning is a powerful tool for maintaining cognitive vitality. Enrolling in courses, attending lectures, or pursuing new educational endeavors helps to keep the brain active, promotes neuroplasticity, and fosters a lifelong commitment to cognitive engagement.

In conclusion, the pursuit of better neurocognitive function involves a combination of lifestyle choices, mental engagement, and targeted interventions.

SENSORY PERFORMANCE REPORT
BLUE • OVERALL SCORE 54

KEY
FIRST EVALUATION — 12/01/2022 @ 13:56
AREA OF INCREASE — PERCENTILE

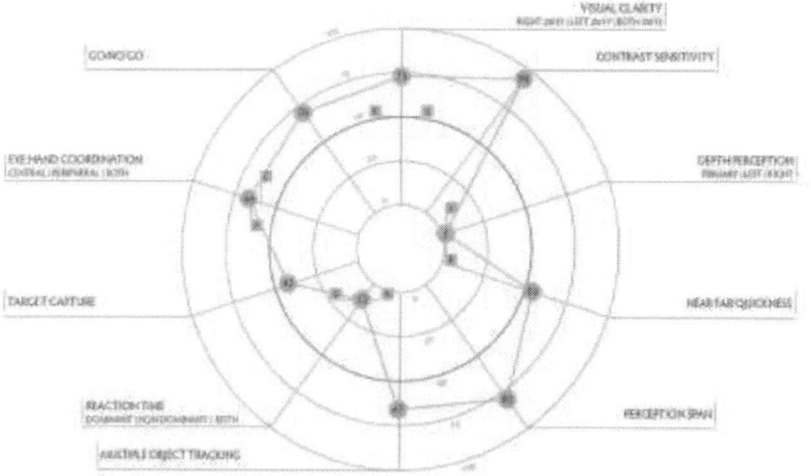

SPORT
AUTO RACING

POSITION
SPORTS CAR

HEIGHT
5'7"

CURRENT LEVEL
PROFESSIONAL/ELITE

COMPARED TO
PROFESSIONAL/ELITE
AUTO RACING
SPORTS CAR

STRENGTHS
CONTRAST SENSITIVITY
PERCEPTION SPAN
GO/NO GO
MULTIPLE OBJECT TRACKING

OPPORTUNITIES
DEPTH PERCEPTION
REACTION TIME
TARGET CAPTURE
VISUAL CLARITY

PRESCRIPTION PLAN
EYE EXAM RECOMMENDED
DEPTH PERCEPTION
DYNAMIC VISION
STROBE EYEWEAR

SENAPTEC

Chapter 5

The Mind-Body Connection: Bridging Mental and Physical Health

---

The intricate relationship between mental and physical health underscores the holistic nature of well-being, where the state of the mind and body are inextricably linked.

The dynamic interplay between mental and physical health has profound implications for an individual's overall quality of life and underscores the importance of adopting a comprehensive approach to healthcare.

Physical health serves as a foundation for mental well-being. Regular exercise, a balanced diet, and sufficient sleep contribute not only to the vitality of the body but also play a pivotal role in supporting positive mental health. Exercise, for instance, triggers the release of endorphins, neurotransmitters that act as natural mood lifters, promoting a sense of well-being and reducing symptoms of anxiety and depression.

Conversely, mental health influences physical health

outcomes. Chronic stress, anxiety, and depression can manifest in physical symptoms, contributing to conditions such as cardiovascular disease, gastrointestinal issues, and compromised immune function. The mind-body connection is evident in the intricate ways in which mental states can influence the physiological responses of the body.

Stress, a common facet of modern life, serves as a poignant example of the interconnectedness of mental and physical health. Chronic stress activates the body's "fight or flight" response, leading to the release of stress hormones such as cortisol. Prolonged exposure to elevated cortisol levels can suppress immune function, making individuals more susceptible to infections and other health challenges.

The link between mental and physical health is further exemplified in psychosomatic disorders, where psychological factors contribute to physical symptoms. Conditions such as irritable bowel syndrome (IBS), tension headaches, and chronic pain often have roots in the intricate interplay between mental and physical well-being.

Health-related behaviors, influenced by both mental and physical factors, play a critical role in overall well-being. Individuals with positive mental health

are more likely to engage in health-promoting behaviors such as regular exercise, a nutritious diet, and adequate sleep. Conversely, mental health challenges can contribute to
unhealthy behaviors, including substance abuse and poor dietary choice's.

Recognizing the interconnected nature of mental and physical health, healthcare providers increasingly advocate for integrated approaches to care. Comprehensive healthcare considers both mental and physical aspects, acknowledging that addressing one aspect without considering the other may yield incomplete outcomes.

The symbiotic relationship between mental and physical health highlights the need for a holistic and integrated approach to well-being. Nurturing mental health positively impacts physical health outcomes, and vice versa. As individuals, healthcare professionals, and societies at large recognize and prioritize this interconnectedness, the potential for fostering optimal health and a higher quality of life becomes more attainable. Integrating mental and physical health strategies not only enhances individual well-being but contributes to the development of a more holistic and effective healthcare paradigm.

Understanding the Interplay

The mind-body connection reflects the intricate relationship between mental and physical health, emphasizing that these two aspects of well-being are not isolated but deeply intertwined. Recognizing the profound impact of thoughts, emotions, and psychological states on physical health opens avenues for holistic approaches to well- being.

1. Biological Pathways
- Stress Response: Mental states, particularly stress and anxiety, activate the body's stress response, releasing hormones like cortisol. Chronic activation of this response can contribute to various physical health issues, including cardiovascular problems and compromised immune function.

- Emotional Impact on Health: Positive emotions, on the other hand, have been associated with improved cardiovascular health, enhanced immune function, and even a potentially longer lifespan. The mind's influence extends to physiological processes, affecting everything from blood pressure to inflammation.

Neuro-Cognitive Training and Emotional Well-being

1. **Stress Reduction**
   - Mindfulness-Based Stress Reduction (MBSR): Incorporating elements of mindfulness and meditation, MBSR has shown effectiveness in reducing stress. Neuro-cognitive training that includes mindfulness practices can help individuals cultivate a more adaptive response to stressors.

   - Neurofeedback for Anxiety: Studies suggest that Neurofeedback, a form of neuro-cognitive training, can be beneficial for individuals experiencing anxiety. By training the brain to regulate its activity, Neurofeedback may contribute to anxiety reduction.

2. **Anxiety Management**
   - Cognitive-Behavioral Therapy (CBT): While not a direct neuro-cognitive training method, CBT is a psychological approach that addresses thought patterns influencing emotions and behaviors. CBT has demonstrated efficacy in managing anxiety

by altering maladaptive cognitive processes.

3. Depression Intervention
- Neuro-Cognitive Training and Depression: Research exploring the impact of neuro-cognitive training on depression is ongoing. Certain cognitive training interventions, especially those addressing cognitive biases and negative thought patterns, show promise in mitigating depressive symptoms.

The Comprehensive Approach to Well-being

1. Integrating Physical Activity
- Exercise and Mental Health: Physical activity is a powerful mediator in the mind-body connection. Regular exercise not only enhances physical health but also contributes to improved mood and cognitive function. Incorporating exercise into neuro-cognitive training regimens can amplify the holistic benefits.

2. Nutrition and Cognitive Health
- Dietary Impact on Mental Health: Nutrition plays a role in both physical and

mental well-being. Diets rich in omega-3 fatty acids, antioxidants, and other nutrients support brain health. Considering nutritional factors alongside neuro-cognitive training provides a comprehensive approach to mental resilience.

Navigating a Balanced Well-being

In conclusion, the mind-body connection underscores the profound impact of mental states on physical health and vice versa. Neuro-cognitive training serves as a valuable tool in this interconnected landscape, offering avenues to manage stress, anxiety, and depression by influencing cognitive processes. Integrating these approaches into a holistic framework that considers physical activity, nutrition, and psychological interventions fosters a balanced well-being, empowering individuals to navigate the intricate interplay between mind and body with resilience and vitality.

SENSORY PERFORMANCE REPORT
INDIGO. OVERALL SCORE 28

SENAPTEC

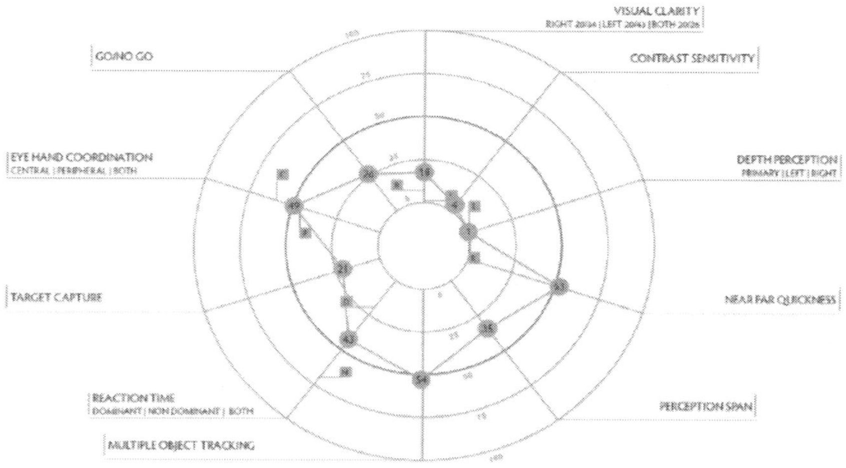

SPORT
AUTO RACING

POSITION
KART

HEIGHT
5'9"

CURRENT LEVEL
HIGH SCHOOL

COMPARED TO
HIGH SCHOOL

STRENGTHS
DYNAMIC
MULTIPLE OBJECT TRACKING
NEAR FAR QUICKNESS
EYE HAND COORDINATION
PERCEPTION SPAN

OPPORTUNITIES
DEPTH PERCEPTION
VISUAL CLARITY
CONTRAST SENSITIVITY
TARGET CAPTURE

PRESCRIPTION PLAN
EYE EXAM RECOMMENDED
DYNAMIC VISION
DEPTH PERCEPTION
PERCEPTION TRAINING

KEY

FIRST EVALUATION — 12/06/2022 @ 21:36

AREA OF INCREASE

PERCENTILE

Chart Labels
- VISUAL CLARITY (RIGHT 20/04 | LEFT 20/63 | BOTH 20/28)
- CONTRAST SENSITIVITY
- DEPTH PERCEPTION (PRIMARY | LEFT | RIGHT)
- NEAR FAR QUICKNESS
- PERCEPTION SPAN
- MULTIPLE OBJECT TRACKING
- REACTION TIME (DOMINANT | NON DOMINANT | BOTH)
- TARGET CAPTURE
- EYE HAND COORDINATION (CENTRAL | PERIPHERAL | BOTH)
- GO/NO GO

Chapter 6

Nutrition and Brain Health: Nourishing the Mind for Optimal Function

Brain health is a multifaceted and crucial aspect of overall well-being, encompassing the intricate workings of the brain that govern cognition, emotion, and behavior. As the epicenter of human experience, maintaining and promoting brain health is essential for a fulfilling and vibrant life.

Central to brain health is cognitive function, encompassing processes such as memory, attention, language, and problem-solving. A sharp and agile mind is vital for navigating daily tasks, engaging in meaningful activities, and adapting to life's challenges. Cognitive vitality is nurtured through mental stimulation, lifelong learning, and activities that challenge and exercise the brain, promoting neuroplasticity—the brain's ability to adapt and reorganize itself.

Regular physical exercise emerges as a cornerstone for maintaining optimal brain health. Exercise promotes increased blood flow to the brain, supports the growth of new neurons, and enhances the release of neurotransmitters that facilitate communication between brain cells. These neurobiological effects contribute to improved cognitive function, including better memory and attention.

The relationship between nutrition and brain health is profound. A balanced diet rich in antioxidants, omega-3 fatty acids, vitamins, and minerals provides the necessary building blocks for brain function. Certain foods, such as fatty fish, berries, nuts, and leafy greens, have been linked to cognitive benefits and a reduced risk of neurodegenerative conditions.

Adequate and quality sleep plays a pivotal role in supporting brain health. During sleep, the brain consolidates memories, processes emotions, and undergoes essential repair and maintenance. Chronic sleep deprivation is associated with cognitive impairments, emphasizing the importance of prioritizing a consistent and restorative sleep routine.

Chronic stress can have detrimental effects on the brain, impacting cognitive function and contributing to mental health challenges. Effective stress management techniques, such as mindfulness meditation, deep breathing exercises, and engaging in relaxing activities, promote resilience and protect the brain from the harmful effects of prolonged stress.

Social engagement is another key factor in maintaining brain health. Meaningful social interactions stimulate the brain, contribute to emotional well-being, and provide a protective buffer against cognitive decline. Strong social connections have been linked to a lower risk of developing neurodegenerative conditions.

The intricate relationship between mental health and brain function highlights the importance of addressing mental health challenges. Conditions such as depression and anxiety can impact cognitive function, and conversely, cognitive decline may contribute to mental health issues. A holistic approach to brain health involves addressing both cognitive and emotional well-being.

Prioritizing brain health is a fundamental investment in one's overall quality of life. From engaging in activities that stimulate cognitive function to adopting lifestyle habits that support physical and mental well-being, individuals can take proactive steps to promote brain resilience. As research continues to uncover the complexities of the brain, fostering a culture that values and prioritizes brain health is integral to creating a society that thrives intellectually, emotionally, and cognitively.

The Intricate Connection: Diet and Cognitive Function

The profound connection between diet and cognitive function highlights the critical role nutrition plays in maintaining optimal brain health. The brain, as a highly metabolically active organ, relies on a constant supply of nutrients to support its functions, including memory, attention, and problem-solving skills.

1. **Nutrient Influence on Brain Structure**
   - Omega-3 Fatty Acids: Found in fatty fish, flaxseeds, and walnuts, omega-3 fatty acids are integral to brain structure and function. They contribute to the formation of cell membranes and play a role in neurotransmitter function, influencing cognitive processes.

   - Antioxidants: Fruits and vegetables rich in antioxidants, such as berries and leafy greens, protect the brain from oxidative stress. This is crucial as the brain is particularly susceptible to damage from free radicals, which can contribute to cognitive decline.

2. Impact on Neurotransmitters

- Protein-Rich Foods: Amino acids from protein-rich foods like lean meats, dairy, and legumes are precursors to neurotransmitters. These chemical messengers play a pivotal role in communication between brain cells, influencing mood, motivation, and cognitive function.

- Complex Carbohydrates: Whole grains, fruits, and vegetables provide a steady supply of glucose, the brain's primary energy source. Maintaining stable blood glucose levels supports sustained attention and prevents cognitive fatigue.

3. Micronutrients and Cognitive Health

- Vitamins and Minerals: Essential vitamins and minerals, including B-vitamins, vitamin D, and zinc, contribute to cognitive health. They support various processes such as the production of neurotransmitters, DNA repair, and overall brain function.

Recommended Foods for Brain Health

1. Fatty Fish
Rich in omega-3 fatty acids, fish like salmon, trout, and sardines support brain structure and function.

2. Berries
Packed with antioxidants, berries (blueberries, strawberries) help protect the brain from oxidative stress.

3. Leafy Greens
Spinach, kale, and other leafy greens provide a wealth of vitamins, minerals, and antioxidants crucial for brain health.

4. Nuts and Seeds
Walnuts, flaxseeds, and chia seeds are excellent sources of omega-3 fatty acids, promoting cognitive function.

5. Lean Proteins
Chicken, turkey, eggs, and legumes provide amino acids essential for neurotransmitter synthesis.

6. Whole Grains
Foods like brown rice, quinoa, and oats offer complex carbohydrates, sustaining steady glucose

levels for optimal brain energy.

7. Colorful Vegetables
Vegetables like bell peppers, broccoli, and sweet potatoes provide a variety of vitamins and minerals crucial for cognitive health.

Strategies for a Brain-Boosting Diet

1. Balanced and Varied Diet
Adopting a well-rounded diet that includes a variety of nutrient-dense foods ensures a broad spectrum of essential nutrients.

2. Hydration
Staying adequately hydrated is vital for cognitive function. Dehydration can impair concentration and increase the perception of task difficulty.

3. Moderation and Avoidance
Moderating the intake of processed foods high in sugar and saturated fats helps prevent inflammation, which can negatively impact cognitive health.

The Journey to Cognitive Well-being

In conclusion, the connection between nutrition and brain health is a crucial element in the pursuit of cognitive well-being. Choosing foods that support brain function and maintaining a balanced, nutrient-rich diet contribute to cognitive resilience and may even reduce the risk of age-related cognitive decline. Nurturing the mind through thoughtful dietary choices is a powerful strategy for unlocking the full potential of cognitive function and fostering overall well-being.

SENSORY PERFORMANCE REPORT

VIOLET • OVERALL SCORE 30

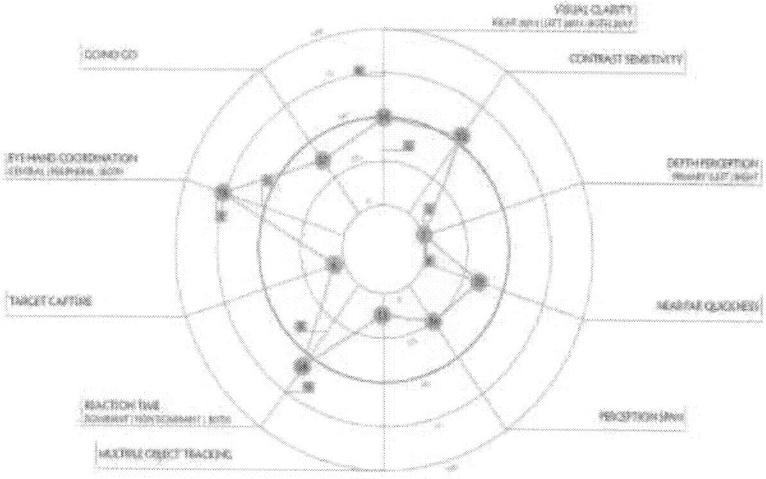

SPORT
AUTO RACING

POSITION
STOCK CAR

HEIGHT
5'10"

CURRENT LEVEL
PROFESSIONAL/ELITE

COMPARED TO
PROFESSIONAL/ELITE
AUTO RACING
STOCK CAR

STRENGTHS
EYE HAND COORDINATION
CONTRAST SENSITIVITY
GO/NO GO
NEAR FAR QUICKNESS

OPPORTUNITIES
DEPTH PERCEPTION
TARGET CAPTURE
MULTIPLE OBJECT TRACKING
VISUAL CLARITY

PRESCRIPTION PLAN
DYNAMIC VISION
DEPTH PERCEPTION
NEAR FAR SHIFT
PERCEPTION TRAINING

KEY
- FIRST EVALUATION 12/02/2022 @ 10:52
- PERCENTILE
- AREA OF INCREASE

SENAPTEC

Chapter 7

Enhancing Cognitive Fitness: The Synergistic Impact of Physical Activity and Cognitive Training.

This chapter explores the multifaceted relationship between physical activity, cognitive fitness, and their combined impact on overall well-being. Examining the extensive body of research, we delve into the specific benefits of exercise on the brain and investigate how integrating cognitive training with physical activity can amplify these effects, offering a holistic approach to mental resilience and overall health.

The integration of physical and cognitive training represents a holistic approach to overall well-being, recognizing the intricate connection between physical fitness and cognitive function. This synergistic combination goes beyond the conventional separation of physical exercise and mental stimulation, offering a comprehensive strategy that enhances both the body and the mind.

Physical exercise has long been acknowledged for its positive impact on cognitive function. Aerobic activities, strength training, and flexibility exercises not only contribute to cardiovascular health and muscular strength but also stimulate the release of neurotransmitters and growth factors that support brain health. Regular exercise has been associated with improved memory, attention, and executive functions.

On the cognitive front, engaging in activities that challenge the mind, such as puzzles, memory games, and learning new skills, promotes neuroplasticity—the brain's ability to reorganize and adapt. Cognitive training encourages the formation of new neural connections and the strengthening of existing ones, fostering a resilient and agile mind.

The integration of physical and cognitive training leverages the synergies between these two domains. Activities that combine both elements, such as dance, martial arts, or interactive video games, require coordination, concentration, and memory recall.

This dual-tasking approach enhances the cognitive demands of the exercise, leading to a more comprehensive and impactful training experience.

Combining physical and cognitive training can amplify neuroplasticity. For instance, incorporating cognitive challenges into a workout routine, such as solving problems or making decisions during physical activities, can enhance the brain's adaptive capabilities. This integrated approach not only improves specific cognitive functions but also contributes to a more resilient and adaptable brain.

The combined approach to physical and cognitive training is valuable at every stage of life. In children and adolescents, it supports healthy brain development and academic performance. For adults, it can enhance productivity, cognitive vitality, and overall well-being. In older adults, this integrated approach becomes a potent tool in mitigating age-related cognitive decline and reducing the risk of neurodegenerative conditions.

The practicality of combining physical and cognitive training extends beyond the gym or workout space. Improved cognitive functions, such as enhanced attention and multitasking abilities, have real-world applications, facilitating better performance in academic, professional, and daily life activities. This approach nurtures a holistic skill set that is beneficial across various domains.

The key to a successful integration of physical and cognitive training lies in creating sustainable habits. Tailoring activities to personal preferences, incorporating variety into routines, and ensuring gradual progression contribute to adherence. The enjoyment derived from the combination of physical and cognitive challenges promotes a positive feedback loop, fostering continued engagement over the long term.

The amalgamation of physical and cognitive training represents a dynamic and synergistic approach to overall health. By recognizing the interconnectedness of the body and mind, individuals can leverage this combination to maximize the benefits for both physical fitness and cognitive function. As research continues to explore the nuances of this integrated approach, it offers a promising avenue for individuals seeking a comprehensive and effective strategy to promote their well-being across the lifespan.

Cognitive fitness, encompassing memory, attention, and problem-solving skills, is a vital component of overall well-being. Physical activity has long been recognized for its myriad health benefits, but recent research illuminates its profound impact on cognitive function. This paper aims to elucidate the cognitive benefits of exercise and explore the synergistic effects of combining physical and cognitive training on the holistic well-being of individuals.

The Benefits of Exercise on the Brain

1. Neuroplasticity and Structural Changes: Physical activity has been linked to enhanced neuroplasticity, promoting the formation of new neural connections and the growth of neurons, particularly in brain regions associated with learning and memory.

2. Neurotransmitter Release: Exercise triggers the release of neurotransmitters such as dopamine and serotonin, contributing to improved mood, reduced stress, and enhanced cognitive function.

3. Vascular Health: Regular physical activity supports cardiovascular health, ensuring optimal blood flow to the brain. Improved vascular health is associated with a lower risk of cognitive decline and

neurodegenerative diseases.

The Role of Cognitive Training

1. Cognitive Resilience: Cognitive training involves activities that challenge and stimulate the brain, fostering cognitive resilience. Engaging in cognitive exercises, such as puzzles and memory games, enhances neural networks and cognitive flexibility.

2. Attention and Focus: Specific cognitive training can improve attention and focus, crucial components of cognitive function. Techniques like mindfulness meditation have been shown to positively impact cognitive control.

The Synergistic Impact

1. Enhanced Cognitive Performance: Studies suggest that combining physical and cognitive training results in superior cognitive performance compared to engaging in either activity alone. The synergistic effect manifests in improved

memory, attention, and executive functions.

2. Mood and Stress Regulation: The combination of physical and cognitive training contributes to a more robust stress response system. Individuals often experience better mood regulation and reduced stress levels, providing a comprehensive approach to mental well-being.

3. Long-Term Cognitive Health: Integrating both forms of training may contribute to long-term cognitive health, potentially reducing the risk of age- related cognitive decline and neurodegenerative disorders.

This section provides practical insights into how individuals can incorporate both physical and cognitive training into their routines. It discusses personalized exercise plans, cognitive exercises, and the importance of variety for comprehensive cognitive well-being.

In conclusion, the combination of physical activity and cognitive training emerges as a potent strategy for enhancing cognitive fitness and overall well-being.

Recognizing the interconnectedness of body and mind opens avenues for personalized approaches to mental resilience. As we navigate the dynamic landscape of cognitive health, this integrated approach stands as a promising frontier for individuals seeking to optimize their cognitive function and thrive in all aspects of life.

SENSORY PERFORMANCE REPORT
PINK • OVERALL SCORE 29

SENAPTEC

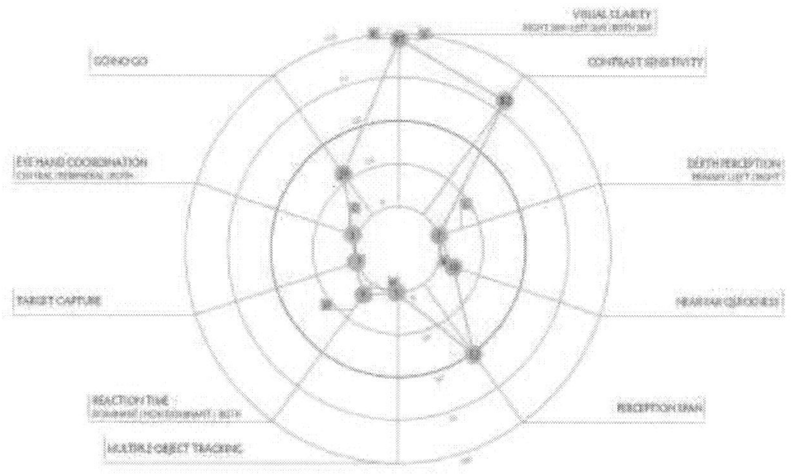

KEY
- FIRST EVALUATION — 05/04/2022 @ 20:58
- AREA OF INCREASE
- PERCENTILE

SPORT
AUTO RACING

POSITION
KART

HEIGHT
4'0"

CURRENT LEVEL
MIDDLE SCHOOL

COMPARED TO
MIDDLE SCHOOL
DYNAMIC

STRENGTHS
VISUAL CLARITY
CONTRAST SENSITIVITY
PERCEPTION SPAN GO/NO GO

OPPORTUNITIES
DEPTH PERCEPTION MULTIPLE OBJECT TRACKING/TARGET CAPTURE
EYE HAND COORDINATION

PRESCRIPTION PLAN
DYNAMIC VISION
NEAR FAR SHIFT
DEPTH PERCEPTION
STROBE EYEWEAR

Chapter 8

Sleep and Brain Restoration: Unlocking the Power of Quality Rest

Sleep is a fundamental aspect of human physiology, playing a crucial role in physical health, mental well-being, and cognitive function. This information paper explores the importance of quality sleep, shedding light on its profound impact on brain restoration and cognitive recovery. Additionally, it provides practical strategies for improving sleep hygiene to optimize brain health.

Brain restoration is a concept that encapsulates the strategies and interventions aimed at rejuvenating and revitalizing the brain's structure and function. In the face of challenges such as stress, aging, or neurological conditions, the pursuit of brain restoration has become a focal point in the field of neuroscience, offering hope for improved cognitive function and overall well-being.

At the heart of brain restoration lies the remarkable

concept of neuroplasticity. The brain's ability to reorganize itself in response to experience and environmental changes enables adaptation and recovery. Neural connections can be strengthened, new pathways can be formed, and damaged areas may find alternative routes for function. This inherent plasticity provides the foundation for brain restoration efforts.

Physical exercise stands out as a powerful catalyst for brain restoration. Regular aerobic exercise has been linked to increased hippocampal volume, the region associated with memory and learning. Exercise promotes the release of neurotrophic factors, such as brain-derived neurotrophic factor (BDNF), which supports the growth and maintenance of neurons, fostering a conducive environment for brain restoration.

Cognitive training, involving activities that challenge and stimulate the mind, plays a vital role in brain restoration. Engaging in puzzles, memory games, Elite Lab Stix and learning new skills encourages the formation of new neural connections. These cognitive exercises not only enhance specific cognitive functions but also contribute to overall brain health, promoting restoration and adaptation.

Nutrition plays a crucial role in brain restoration. A diet rich in antioxidants, omega-3 fatty acids, vitamins, and minerals provides essential nutrients that support brain function and protect against oxidative stress. Certain foods, such as blueberries, fish, nuts, and dark leafy greens, have been associated with cognitive benefits, contributing to the restoration of optimal brain health.

Quality sleep is a cornerstone of brain restoration. During sleep, the brain undergoes processes essential for cognitive recovery, including memory consolidation and the removal of toxins. Adequate and restful sleep supports overall brain health, promoting resilience and enhancing the brain's capacity for restoration.

Chronic stress can have detrimental effects on the brain, impacting cognitive function and hindering restoration. Stress reduction techniques, such as mindfulness meditation, deep breathing exercises, and relaxation practices, contribute to emotional well-being and create an environment conducive to brain restoration.

Advancements in neuroscience have led to the exploration of innovative technologies and therapies for brain restoration. Neurofeedback, transcranial magnetic stimulation (TMS), and virtual reality interventions show promise in enhancing cognitive functions and facilitating neural recovery. These approaches offer novel avenues for individuals seeking targeted brain restoration.

The pursuit of lifelong learning and intellectual engagement contributes to ongoing brain restoration. Staying intellectually active through activities such as reading, attending lectures, and participating in stimulating conversations fosters cognitive vitality and resilience, supporting the brain's adaptive capacities.

The concept of brain restoration embodies the dynamic nature of the brain's capacity for recovery and adaptation. By embracing a multifaceted approach that incorporates physical exercise, cognitive training, nutrition, sleep, stress reduction, and emerging technologies, individuals can proactively contribute to the restoration of their brain health. This holistic perspective not only fosters cognitive recovery but also empowers individuals to lead fulfilling and vibrant lives across the lifespan.

The Importance of Quality Sleep

1. Memory Consolidation: During sleep, the

brain consolidates and organizes memories, facilitating learning and information retention. Quality sleep is integral to the conversion of short-term memories into long-term storage.

2. Neuroplasticity: Sleep supports neuroplasticity, the brain's ability to adapt and reorganize itself. This process is crucial for learning new skills, adapting to experiences, and maintaining cognitive flexibility.

3. Emotional Regulation: Adequate sleep contributes to emotional resilience by regulating mood and stress levels. Insufficient sleep has been linked to heightened emotional reactivity and an increased risk of mood disorders.

4. Physical Restoration: Sleep is a time for the body and brain to undergo physical restoration. Cellular repair, hormone regulation, and immune system function are all processes facilitated during sleep, contributing to overall health.

Strategies for Improving Sleep and Cognitive Recovery Consistent

Sleep Schedule
Establish a regular sleep-wake cycle by going to bed and waking up at the same
time every day, even on weekends. Consistency reinforces the body's internal
clock.

Create a Relaxing Bedtime Routine
Develop calming pre-sleep rituals such as reading a book, practicing relaxation techniques, or taking a warm bath. These activities signal to the body that it's time to wind down.

Optimize Sleep Environment
Ensure the sleep environment is conducive to rest. This includes a comfortable mattress and pillows, adequate room darkness, and a cool temperature.

Limit Screen Time Before Bed
Exposure to blue light from screens can interfere with the production of the sleep- inducing hormone melatonin. Limit screen time at least an hour before bedtime.

Mindfulness and Relaxation Techniques
Practices like mindfulness meditation and deep

breathing exercises can calm the mind, making it easier to transition into a restful sleep.

Manage Stress and Anxiety
Implement stress-management strategies, such as journaling, yoga, or talking to a mental health professional, to alleviate anxiety that might disrupt sleep.

Limit Caffeine and Stimulants
Reduce or eliminate the consumption of caffeine and stimulants in the hours leading up to bedtime. These substances can interfere with the ability to fall asleep.

Regular Exercise
Engage in regular physical activity, but avoid intense workouts close to bedtime. Exercise can promote better sleep by reducing stress and anxiety.

Quality sleep is a cornerstone of cognitive health, influencing memory, emotional well-being, and overall brain function. By understanding the importance of sleep and implementing effective strategies for improving sleep hygiene, individuals can optimize cognitive recovery, enhance learning and memory, and promote overall well- being. As we unlock the power of quality rest, we embark on a journey towards a more vibrant and resilient mind.

SENSORY PERFORMANCE REPORT
WHITE • OVERALL SCORE 38

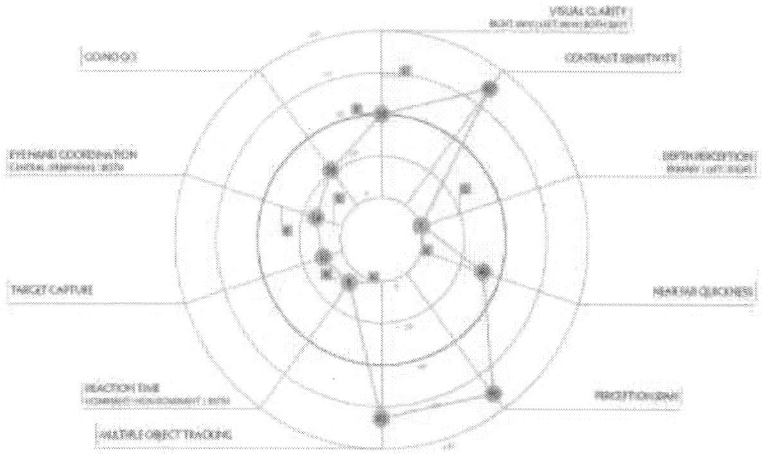

SPORT
AUTO RACING

POSITION
KART

HEIGHT
5'9"

CURRENT LEVEL
HIGH SCHOOL

COMPARED TO
HIGH SCHOOL
DYNAMIC

STRENGTHS
PERCEPTION SPAN
CONTRAST SENSITIVITY
MULTIPLE OBJECT TRACKING
NEAR FAR QUICKNESS

OPPORTUNITIES
DEPTH PERCEPTION
REACTION TIME
TARGET CAPTURE
EYE HAND COORDINATION

PRESCRIPTION PLAN
DYNAMIC VISION
DEPTH PERCEPTION
NEAR FAR SHIFT
STROBE EYEWEAR

KEY

FIRST EVALUATION — 05/04/2022 @ 21:32

AREA OF INCREASE

PERCENTILE

SENAPTEC

Chapter 9

Cognitive Customization for Healthier Longevity

Age-related cognitive changes vary, but common aspects include slower processing speed, reduced working memory, and changes in attention. Tailoring neuro-cognitive training involves adapting exercises to match specific cognitive strengths and challenges at different life stages. For example, focusing on memory enhancement for older adults or attention-building exercises for children. Customizing intensity and complexity is crucial to suit cognitive abilities at each stage.

Cognitive changes throughout the lifespan are a natural and dynamic aspect of human development, reflecting the intricate interplay between biological, environmental, and experiential factors. From infancy to old age, individuals undergo a series of cognitive transformations that shape their abilities, perceptions, and interactions with the world.

The journey of cognitive development begins in

infancy, marked by rapid and foundational changes. Infants gradually acquire basic sensory and motor skills, laying the groundwork for cognitive abilities. The development of object permanence, memory, and the emergence of language skills are pivotal milestones during early childhood. Caregiver interactions and environmental stimuli play crucial roles in shaping cognitive capacities during these formative years.

Middle childhood and adolescence witness further cognitive advancements. The capacity for abstract thinking and problem-solving expands during these stages. Cognitive abilities related to memory, attention, and executive functions continue to mature. Formal education and exposure to diverse experiences contribute to the development of complex cognitive skills, such as critical thinking and decision- making.

Cognitive changes persist into adulthood, characterized by a combination of growth and stabilization. While certain cognitive functions may peak in early adulthood, others, such as wisdom and expertise, may continue to evolve. Experiences, ongoing learning, and occupational demands contribute to cognitive adaptation and resilience.

Additionally, adults may face challenges such as multitasking demands and changes in memory performance, reflecting the nuanced trajectory of cognitive changes.

The later stages of adulthood bring about distinctive cognitive changes. Aging is associated with a decline in some cognitive domains, particularly processing speed and episodic memory. However, other cognitive abilities, such as semantic memory and crystallized intelligence, may remain stable or even improve. Environmental factors, health status, and lifestyle choices influence the trajectory of cognitive aging. Engaging in mentally stimulating activities and maintaining social connections are associated with cognitive resilience in older age.

Throughout the lifespan, the concept of neuroplasticity underscores the brain's capacity to adapt and reorganize. Neural connections can be strengthened, and new ones can be formed in response to experiences and learning. While there are sensitive periods for certain cognitive developments, the brain retains a degree of plasticity, allowing for ongoing adaptation.

Lifestyle factors, including nutrition, exercise, and mental stimulation, significantly influence cognitive changes. Regular physical activity has been linked to cognitive benefits, while a balanced diet rich In nutrients supports brain health. Intellectual engagement, such as continued learning and challenging cognitive activities, contributes to cognitive vitality across the lifespan.

Cognitive health can be improved across the lifespan through various strategies:

1. Regular Exercise: Physical activity enhances blood flow to the brain, promoting cognitive function.

2. Healthy Diet: Nutrient-rich foods, like fruits, vegetables, and omega-3 fatty acids, support brain health.

3. Adequate Sleep: Quality sleep is vital for cognitive performance and memory consolidation.

4. Mental Stimulation: Engage in activities that challenge the brain, such as puzzles, learning new skills, or intellectual pursuits.

5. Social Interaction: Regular socializing can positively impact cognitive health by reducing

stress and promoting emotional well-being.

6. Stress Management: Chronic stress can negatively affect cognitive function, so adopting stress-reduction techniques is essential.

7. Cognitive Training: Activities targeting specific cognitive skills, such as memory or attention exercises, can help maintain and improve cognitive function.

8. Regular Health Checkups: Monitoring and managing overall health, including cardiovascular health, can contribute to cognitive well-being.

9. Avoiding Harmful Substances: Limiting alcohol intake and avoiding tobacco and recreational drugs can protect cognitive function.

10. Lifelong Learning: Embracing a mindset of continuous learning and intellectual curiosity supports cognitive health throughout life.

Tailoring these strategies to individual preferences and life stages enhances their effectiveness in promoting cognitive well-being.

SENSORY PERFORMANCE REPORT
BLACK • OVERALL SCORE 78

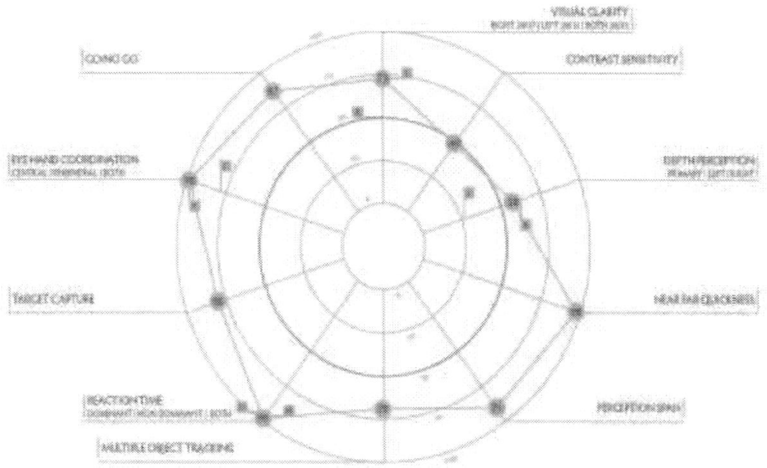

SPORT
AUTO RACING

POSITION
FORMULA

HEIGHT
5'9"

CURRENT LEVEL
PROFESSIONAL/ELITE

COMPARED TO
PROFESSIONAL/ELITE
AUTO RACING
FORMULA

STRENGTHS
NEAR FAR QUICKNESS
EYE HAND COORDINATION
REACTION TIME
PERCEPTION SPAN

OPPORTUNITIES
CONTRAST SENSITIVITY
DEPTH PERCEPTION
VISUAL CLARITY
MULTIPLE OBJECT TRACKING

PRESCRIPTION PLAN
DEPTH PERCEPTION
STROBE EYEWEAR
DYNAMIC VISION
NEAR FAR SHIFT

KEY

FIRST EVALUATION
12/08/2022 @ 21:27

AREA OF INCREASE

PERCENTILE

SENAPTEC

Chapter 10

Integrating Cognitive Training into Your Life

Here are some great training tools to help integrate these concepts into your everyday life.

Incorporating cognitive training into everyday life has become increasingly recognized as a proactive approach to promoting mental agility and resilience. The advent of innovative tools like the Elite Lab Stix offers a convenient and effective way to integrate cognitive training seamlessly into daily routines, unlocking the potential for enhanced cognitive function and overall well-being.

Cognitive training involves exercises and activities designed to challenge and stimulate the brain, fostering the development and maintenance of cognitive abilities. The Elite Lab Stix, with its interactive and engaging features, emerges as a valuable tool for individuals seeking to incorporate cognitive training into their daily lives.

One of the key advantages of the Elite Lab Stix is its ability to seamlessly integrate into daily routines. Whether during a coffee break, commuting, or in moments of downtime, the Stix provides quick and accessible cognitive exercises. This ease of integration eliminates barriers to consistent engagement, making cognitive training a natural part of everyday life.

The Elite Lab Stix offers a diverse range of cognitive challenges, targeting various cognitive domains. From memory exercises and problem-solving tasks to attention and pattern recognition activities, users can tailor their cognitive training based on individual preferences and areas of interest. This versatility ensures a well-rounded approach to cognitive stimulation.

The Stix's built-in progress tracking features empower users to monitor their cognitive development over time. This personalized feedback provides insights into strengths and areas for improvement, motivating individuals to stay committed to their cognitive training regimen. The ability to track progress fosters a sense of accomplishment and encourages continued engagement.

Utilizing gamification elements, the Elite Lab Stix transforms cognitive training into an enjoyable and motivating experience. Points, rewards, and interactive challenges create a sense of achievement and make the training process inherently engaging. This gamified approach transforms cognitive exercises into a positive and rewarding aspect of daily life.

The Stix's modular design allows users to select training modules that align with their cognitive goals. Whether focusing on memory enhancement, attention improvement, or problem-solving skills, individuals can customize their training sessions to address specific cognitive needs. This flexibility accommodates varying preferences and evolving cognitive priorities.

Cognitive training with the Elite Lab Stix is not limited by age. From students aiming to boost academic performance to older adults seeking to maintain cognitive vitality, the Stix caters to a diverse audience. This inclusivity underscores the potential for cognitive training to be a lifelong practice, contributing to sustained cognitive health across different life stages.

Incorporating cognitive training into everyday life using tools like the Elite Lab Stix represents a paradigm shift in how individuals approach mental well-being. By seamlessly integrating cognitive exercises into daily routines, individuals can foster cognitive resilience, enhance specific cognitive skills, and ultimately contribute to a more agile and adaptive mind. As technology continues to advance, the accessibility and effectiveness of cognitive training tools empower individuals to take an active role in nurturing their cognitive health, paving the way for a future where mental well- being is an integral part of daily life.

Integrating Cognitive Training

1. Mindful Meditation: Incorporate mindfulness exercises into your daily routine to enhance focus and reduce stress.

2. Brain Games and Apps: Use cognitive training apps or games that challenge memory, problem-solving, and critical thinking skills.

3. Learn Something New: Engage in lifelong learning, whether it's a new language,

musical instrument, or a hobby that stimulates your mind.

4. Physical Exercise: Regular physical activity boosts cognitive function, so include exercises that get your heart pumping in your routine.

5. Balanced Diet: Nutrient-rich foods, especially those high in omega-3 fatty acids and antioxidants, support brain health.

6. Adequate Sleep: Prioritize quality sleep to consolidate memories and promote overall cognitive well-being.

7. Social Connections: Maintain social interactions to stimulate cognitive function and emotional well-being.

Creating a Holistic Wellness Plan:

1. Assess Your Current Health: Identify areas of improvement in physical, mental, and emotional well-being.

2. Set Realistic Goals: Establish achievable

targets for different aspects of your life, such as fitness, nutrition, and stress management.

3. Balanced Nutrition: Develop a meal plan with a variety of nutrients, focusing on whole foods and adequate hydration.

4. Regular Exercise: Include a mix of cardiovascular, strength training, and flexibility exercises in your routine.

5. Mind-Body Practices: Integrate activities like yoga or tai chi to promote the connection between mental and physical well-being.

6. Stress Management: Implement stress-reducing techniques such as deep breathing, meditation, or mindfulness.

7. Quality Sleep: Establish a consistent sleep schedule and create a conducive sleep environment.

8. Regular Health Check-ups: Schedule routine health check-ups to monitor your physical

health and address any concerns promptly.

9. Social Support: Cultivate positive relationships and seek support from friends, family, or community groups.

10. Continuous Evaluation: Periodically review and adjust your wellness plan to align with changing priorities and lifestyle adjustments.

SENSORY PERFORMANCE REPORT
BROWN • OVERALL SCORE 42

KEY
- FIRST EVALUATION — 11/19/2023 @ 22:18
- AREA OF INCREASE
- PERCENTILE

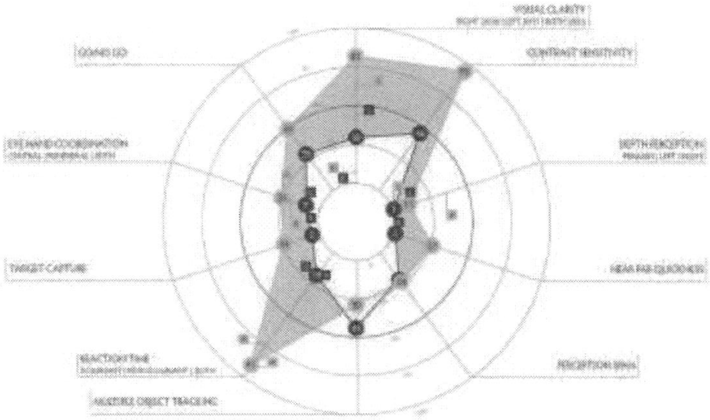

SPORT
FOOTBALL (AMERICAN)

POSITION
WIDE RECEIVER

HEIGHT
14

CURRENT LEVEL
MIDDLE SCHOOL

COMPARED TO
MIDDLE SCHOOL
FOOTBALL (AMERICAN)
BALL HANDLER

STRENGTHS
CONTRAST SENSITIVITY
REACTION TIME
VISUAL CLARITY
GO/NO GO

OPPORTUNITIES
DEPTH PERCEPTION
EYE HAND COORDINATION
PERCEPTION SPAN
TARGET CAPTURE

PRESCRIPTION PLAN
SECOND EVALUATION
DYNAMIC VISION DEPTH PERCEPTION
PERCEPTION TRAINING
NEAR FAR SHIFT

SENAPTEC

Chapter 11

Success Stories

One example is the case of a stroke survivor who used neuro-cognitive training to improve memory, attention, and problem-solving skills. Through targeted exercises and activities, this individual experienced enhanced cognitive abilities, contributing to a better quality of life post-stroke.

Additionally, students with learning disabilities have benefited from neuro-cognitive training, showing improvements in academic performance and overall cognitive function.

In a classroom setting, neuro-cognitive training has shown success in improving students' focus, memory, and academic performance. For instance, a teacher implemented cognitive exercises and brain training activities in the classroom, which resulted in increased attention spans and better retention of information among students. This approach has also been beneficial for students with attention disorders, helping them better engage with lessons and ultimately contributing to a more positive learning experience.

In conclusion, neuro-cognitive training has demonstrated its efficacy in various contexts, from aiding stroke survivors in reclaiming cognitive function to enhancing academic performance in students.

These success stories underscore the potential of targeted cognitive exercises to positively impact individuals' memory, attention, and problem-solving skills. While further research is needed to refine and tailor these approaches, the current evidence suggests that neuro-cognitive training holds promise as a valuable tool for cognitive enhancement and rehabilitation.

Chapter 12

Impact of Health Avenue Technologies

Emerging technologies and research in cognitive health are paving the way for innovative approaches to neuro-cognitive training. Virtual reality (VR), artificial intelligence (AI), and neurofeedback are among the technologies being explored. VR allows for immersive cognitive exercises, AI enables personalized training programs based on individual needs, and neurofeedback involves real-time monitoring and adjustment of cognitive activities.

The potential Impact of neuro-cognitive training on society is significant. Improved cognitive function can enhance productivity in various fields, from education to the workplace. It holds promise for addressing cognitive decline in aging populations, contributing to better mental health outcomes, and aiding rehabilitation after neurological injuries or conditions. As these technologies advance, the accessibility and effectiveness of neuro-cognitive training may further increase, positively influencing the well-being and cognitive abilities of a broader segment of society.

SENSORY PERFORMANCE REPORT
GRAY · OVERALL SCORE 22

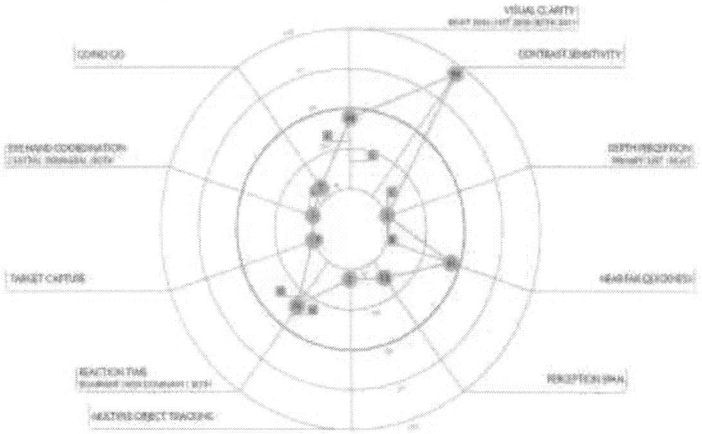

SPORT
AUTO RACING

POSITION
KART

HEIGHT
4'0"

CURRENT LEVEL
MIDDLE SCHOOL

COMPARED TO
MIDDLE SCHOOL

STRENGTHS
DYNAMIC

OPPORTUNITIES
CONTRAST SENSITIVITY
NEAR FAR QUICKNESS
REACTION TIME
VISUAL CLARITY

PRESCRIPTION PLAN
TARGET CAPTURE
EYE HAND COORDINATION
DEPTH PERCEPTION
MULTIPLE OBJECT TRACKING

EYE EXAM RECOMMENDED
DYNAMIC VISION
DEPTH PERCEPTION
PERCEPTION TRAINING

KEY

FIRST EVALUATION — 05/04/2022 @ 22:11

AREA OF INCREASE

PERCENTILE

SENAPTEC

Conclusion

Prioritizing cognitive fitness is essential for a thriving and fulfilled life. Embracing neuro-cognitive training, especially with the advancements in emerging technologies, can empower individuals to enhance memory, focus, and problem-solving skills. Just as we prioritize physical exercise for a healthy body, dedicating time to mental workouts fosters resilience against cognitive decline and promotes overall well-being. As the landscape of cognitive health evolves, investing in our mental acuity becomes an investment in a more vibrant and engaged future.

Executive functioning refers to a set of cognitive processes that enable individuals to manage, plan, and regulate their behavior to achieve goals. The Elite Lab Stix, a cutting-edge tool designed to enhance executive functioning, offers a unique approach to cognitive development.

One key aspect of executive functioning is working memory, the ability to hold and manipulate information in the mind. The Elite Lab

Stix provides engaging exercises that challenge working memory through various tasks, promoting mental agility and strengthening this crucial cognitive skill.

Moreover, the Stix addresses the concept of cognitive flexibility, the ability to adapt and switch between different tasks or mental sets. By presenting users with diverse challenges and problem-solving scenarios, the Elite Lab Stix cultivates flexibility in thinking, fostering adaptability in real-world situations.

In the realm of inhibitory control, the Stix proves to be an invaluable asset. This executive function involves suppressing impulses and distractions, allowing for sustained focus on a given task. Through interactive exercises, the Stix hones users' ability to filter out irrelevant information, promoting sharper attention and improved inhibitory control.

Planning and organization are vital components of executive functioning, and the Elite Lab Stix excels in cultivating these skills. Users engage in structured activities that require strategic thinking and the development of plans, encouraging effective organization and goal-directed behavior.

Furthermore, the Stix enhances time management skills, a critical aspect of executive functioning. By incorporating timed challenges and tasks, users learn to allocate their time efficiently and develop a heightened awareness of deadlines—a valuable skill applicable to both academic and professional settings.

In conclusion, the Elite Lab Stix emerges as an innovative tool for bolstering executive functioning. Its multidimensional approach, encompassing working memory, cognitive flexibility, inhibitory control, planning, organization, and time management, makes it a comprehensive solution for individuals seeking to enhance their cognitive abilities. As we navigate an increasingly complex and fast-paced world, tools like the Elite Lab Stix play a pivotal role in empowering individuals to succeed in various aspects of their lives.

ELITE LAB STIX
NEW AT ELITE PERFORMANCE

ELITE LAB STIX

Uses for the Elite Lab stix include:
- Increase in expressive and receptive communication
- Proprioception- overall awareness of the body in space
- Reduced latency
- Bi-lateral motor coordination. The ability to use both hands and to cross the midline.
- Increase social skills
- Executive functioning

$35

Contact info:
elitelabstix@gmail.com
765.499.1005

ELITE PERFORMANCE

Elite Lab Stix QR Codes

Made in the USA
Columbia, SC
23 February 2024

bda84c96-602b-4c10-b8bd-c9015cd88568R02